Build a Website

Marcie Flinchum Atkins

Content Consultant

Sarah Otts
Scratch Online Community Developer
MIT Media Lab, Massachusetts Institute of Technology

Reading Consultant

Jeanne M. Clidas, Ph.D.
Reading Specialist

Children's Press®
An Imprint of Scholastic Inc.

Library of Congress Cataloging-in-Publication Data
Names: Atkins, Marcie Flinchum, author.
Title: Build a website/by Marcie Flinchum Atkins.
Description: New York, NY: Children's Press, an imprint of Scholastic, Inc., [2019] |
Series: Rookie get ready to code | Includes index.
Identifiers: LCCN 2018027248 | ISBN 9780531132265 (library binding) | ISBN 9780531137017 (paperback)
Subjects: LCSH: Web site development—Juvenile literature. | Web sites—Design—Juvenile literature.
Classification: LCC TK5105.888 .A825 2019 | DDC 006.7—dc23

Produced by Spooky Cheetah Press
Creative Direction: Judith E. Christ for Scholastic Inc.
Design: Brenda Jackson

Published in 2019 by Children's Press, an imprint of Scholastic Inc.

Printed in North Mankato, MN, USA   113

SCHOLASTIC, CHILDREN'S PRESS, GET READY TO CODE™, and associated logos are trademarks and/or
registered trademarks of Scholastic Inc.

1 2 3 4 5 6 7 8 9 10 R 28 27 26 25 24 23 22 21 20 19

Scholastic Inc., 557 Broadway, New York, NY 10012.

Photos © cover: JGI/Jamie Grill/Getty Images; cover background: RioAbajoRio/Shutterstock; cover and throughout robots: the8monkey/iStockphoto;
inside cover and throughout: pmmix/Shutterstock; 4-5 dashed lines: Golden Shrimp/Shutterstock; 4 bird: Andegraund548/Dreamstime; 5 top
left: SukanPhoto/Shutterstock; 5 bottom left: 59Olena Markova/Shutterstock; 5 bottom right: MarijaPiliponyte/Shutterstock; 5 smiley face: Vertes
Edmond Mihai/Shutterstock; 6: vgajic/iStockphoto; 6 inset browser: DG-Studio/Shutterstock; 7 explorer: Rose Carson/Shutterstock; 7 chrome:
Rose Carson/Shutterstock; 7 safari: Alamy Images; 7 firefox: Firefox.com; 9 girl at computer: Rawpixel.com/Shutterstock; 9 website template: user
friendly/Shutterstock; 9 school supply background: TV/Shutterstock; 9 school supplies: Green Leaf/Shutterstock; 9 shopping cart: Titov Nikolai/
Shutterstock; 10: OJO_Images/Getty Images; 11 tablet: Andrey_Popov/Shutterstock; 11 web browser: nicemonkey/Shutterstock; 11 web template:
ra2studio/Shutterstock; 11 shark: Natalie11345/Shutterstock; 11 white house: turtix/Shutterstock; 11 children: michaeljung/Shutterstock; 11
windy day: Puerta/Addictive Creative/Offset.com; 13 phone: SukanPhoto/Shutterstock; 13 web template: Lucie Drobna/Shutterstock; 13 dog
with food: Javier Brosch/Shutterstock; 13 dog with leash: Javier Brosch/Shutterstock; 13 dog in leaves: Irina Filkova/Shutterstock; 15, 19 dogs:
Liliya Kulianionak/Shutterstock; 15, 19 dog icons: Rain Art/Shutterstock; 15, 19 browser tabs: moham'ed/Shutterstock; 19 laptop: Lukas Gojda/
Shutterstock; 21 tablet: GE_4530/Shutterstock; 21 dog in leaves: Irina Filkova/Shutterstock; 21 silhouettes: WarmWorld/Shutterstock; 21 comment
bubbles: Ice_AisberG/Shutterstock; 23 top: Rawpixel.com/Shutterstock; 23 bottom: Hor Kosal/EyeEm/Getty Images; 25 top: Andrii Symonenko/
Shutterstock; 25 center: Teguh Jati Prasetyo/Shutterstock; 25 bottom: Teguh Jati Prasetyo/Shutterstock; 27 child with tablet: Gelpi/Shutterstock;
27 web template: Jozsef Bagota/Shutterstock; 27 earth: Lightspring/Shutterstock; 27 tiger: Anna-av/iStockphoto; 27 rhino: JasonPrince/
iStockphoto; 27 elephant: Svetlana Foote/Shutterstock; 27 turtle: ShaneMyersPhoto/iStockphoto; 27 orangutan: David Evison/
Shutterstock; 27 orca: Tory Kallman/Shutterstock; 27 shark: SylwiaDomaradzka/iStockphoto; 27 polar bear: Flinster007/
iStockphoto; 30: nevodka/Shutterstock.

TABLE OF CONTENTS

Chapter 1

The Internet

You can use the Internet to find out almost anything you want to know. Do you want to learn how to tie your shoes? You can learn how to do it on the Internet. Do you want to know the population of Greece? You can find it on the Internet, too. We can also use the Internet to communicate with people close by and far away.

How the Internet Works

message or data sent

1

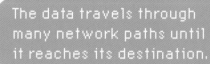

The data travels through many network paths until it reaches its destination.

2

2

2

3

message or data received

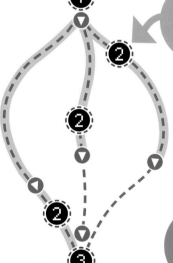

Think About It

What was life like before the Internet?

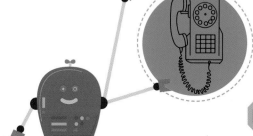

The Internet allows you to look at websites. You can visit them by using a browser. A browser lets you look through—or browse—the Internet. You can find new websites by typing what you are looking for into a search bar.

What browser do you use?

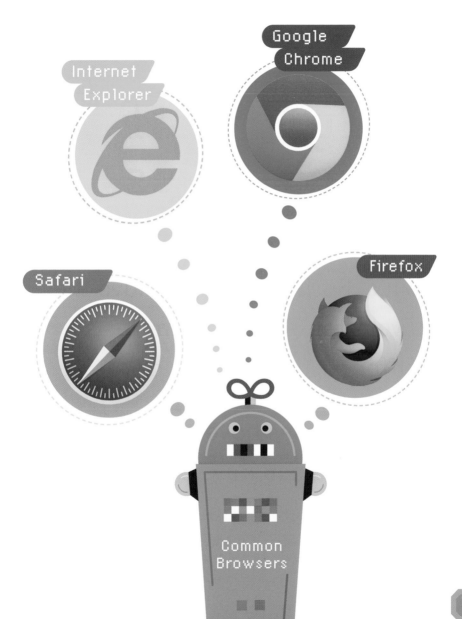

Internet Explorer

Google Chrome

Safari

Firefox

Common Browsers

Chapter 2

Types of Websites

There are many different types of websites. Businesses often have their own websites. A website makes it easier for customers to find them.

Many businesses have shopping websites. You can buy something online. Then it is shipped to your home.

School Supplies On Sale

Home Customer service

Notebook
$ 0.99

Post-its
$1.99

Colored pencils
$3.99

Eraser
$0.49

Compass
$2.99

Calculator
$3.99

View more

View more

View more

Please review our services:

Contact Us:

Our Staff:

shopping website

9

People used to learn about what was going on in the world mainly by reading the newspaper or watching the news on TV. Today a lot of people visit news websites to find this information.

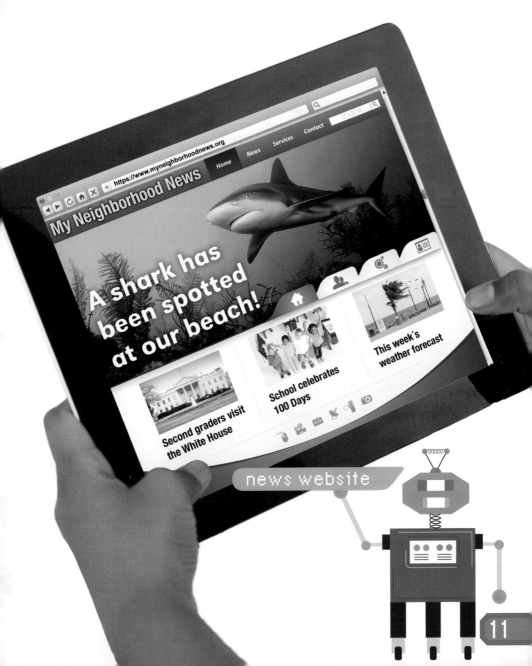

news website

11

Another type of website is a blog. "Blog" is short for "web log." The people who create blogs are called bloggers. Anybody can be a blogger, including you! A blog entry might be an informational article. It could also be a personal story written by the blogger.

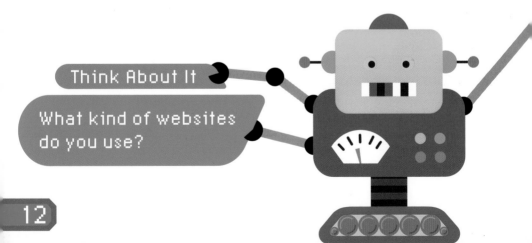

Think About It

What kind of websites do you use?

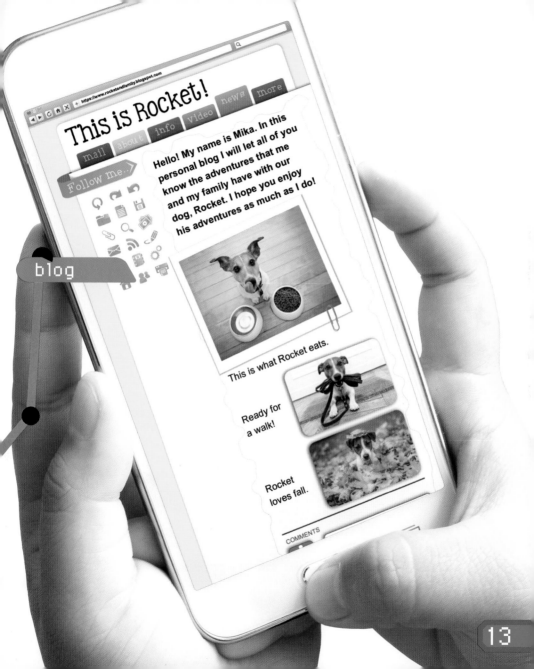

blog

This is Rocket!

mail   about   info   video   news   more

Follow me...

https://www.rocketandfamily.blogspot.com

Hello! My name is Mika. In this personal blog I will let all of you know the adventures that me and my family have with our dog, Rocket. I hope you enjoy his adventures as much as I do!

This is what Rocket eats.

Ready for a walk!

Rocket loves fall.

COMMENTS

13

Chapter 3

Parts of a Website

A website has different parts. The URL (uniform resource locator) is the website address. It tells you how to find that site on the Internet.

Think About It

Does this website have the best URL? Why or why not?

URL

◄ ► ⟳ ⌂ ✕ + https://alldogsforadoption.org 🔍

| Dog Care | Find a Dog | Help Dogs | Contact us | FAQ |

ALL DOGS FOR ADOPTION
Adopt a dog today!

Are you planning to adopt a dog? We can help! We are here to guide you in this beautiful process. We will help you and your family find a dog that is right for you.

A domain is a part of a website's URL. You can tell what type of website you are looking at by the three letters at the end of its URL. The chart on page 17 shows examples of common domains.

If you built your own website, what would your URL be?

Domain	What it means	What kind of websites use it
.edu	Education	Colleges or other schools
.com	Commercial	Businesses that are selling something
.org	Organization	Organizations, such as charities, environmental groups, community clubs
.gov	Government	A U.S. government department
.mil	Military	A U.S. military branch

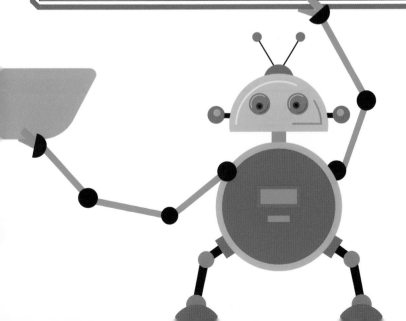

A website's home page is the first page you see. It is the main page of the website. Other pages are linked to the home page.

A home page has a header at the top. It tells you the name of the website and what it is about.

An image and a **logo** also sometimes appear on the home page.

The home page for this site tells you that it is a site for people who want to adopt a dog.

logo

header

https://alldogsforadoption.org

Dog Care | Find a Dog | Help Dogs | Contact us | FAQ

ALL DOGS FOR ADOPTION
Adopt a dog today!

Are you planning to adopt a dog? We can help! We are here to guide you in this beautiful process. We will help you and your family find a dog that is right for you.

Each website lets you **navigate** by clicking on links that lead to other pages.

Many websites have search boxes to help you find a topic on the website.

Blogs usually have a place for reader comments at the bottom of the page.

Rocket loves fall.

COMMENTS

Hi Mika: Rocket is really adorable. I cannot wait to meet him next week.

 REPLY

My dog Bingo also enjoys fall. He loves running outdoors and playing with the leaves. It is hard to convince him to go back home every time we take him out for a walk.

 REPLY

You should bring Rocket to school one day! We could study his cuteness in science class.

 REPLY

blog comments

Coding a Website

A team of people helps build websites. **Programmers** use a special language called **code** to make a website work. Designers focus on how the website looks. They choose colors, **fonts**, and pictures.

Designers decide how the page should look.

WEB DESIGN

LAYOUT

PAGES

Programmers use code to manage how the pages of the website look and act.

Programmers use several different coding languages to make websites.

- HTML (Hypertext Markup Language) helps them develop the layout of the page.

- CSS (Cascading Style Sheet) helps with colors and the location of text.

- JavaScript is used for interactive elements on a page, like forms that are meant to be filled out.

Here are examples of the three coding languages.

HTML

```html
1  <!DOCTYPE html>
2  <html lang="en">
3  <head>
4    <meta charset="UTF-8">
5    <title>Document</title>
6  </head>
7  <body>
8    <main class="container">
9      <section class="features">
10       <div class="feature-item">
```

CSS

```css
body {
    background : #FFF;
    font-size : 12px;
}

a:link, a:visited {
    color: #685966;
    text-decoration : underline;
    font-size : 11px;
}
a:hover {
    color: #2b212c;
}
p {
    margin: 10px 0 10px 0;
    padding: 10px 0 10px 0;
}
```

JavaScript

```javascript
/**
 * Receives array or numbers bugger than 0
 */

function getMaxValue (array) {
    // Declare a new variable to hold maximum value
    var maxValue = 0;

    // Iterate over array's elements
    for (var index=0; index<array.length; index++){

        // get array element at specific index
        var element = array[index];

    }
```

25

You do not need to know code to build a basic website. Programmers build special sites to help you. You can click on buttons to change text. You can add pictures. These website-building programs use WYSIWYG (pronounced WIZZY-WIG). That stands for What You See Is What You Get. It means you can see what the page will look like as you create it.

Now you know how a website is created! What kind of website would you build? Look at the photo on page 27 for fun ideas!

Let's Save These Animals!

Diversity on our planet is very important. We need to do everything we can to preserve it. Let's learn about all the animals on our planet that are at risk of becoming extinct. They need our help!

pictures

text

| ABOUT | WHAT CAN YOU DO? | WHO IS ALREADY HELPING | CONTACT ME |

TIGERS

RHINOCEROSES

ELEPHANTS

SEA TURTLES

ORANGUTANS

ORCAS

GREAT WHITE SHARKS

POLAR BEARS

STORYBOARDING A HOME PAGE

Before building a website, you need a plan. You need to create a storyboard or sketch of your website. Pretend you are going to create a shopping website. You are going to sell clothes that do not fit you anymore. Make sure the website gives your customers all the information they need to purchase your clothes.

▶ **Materials Needed:** plain paper or graph paper, pencil

① Make a list of information to include on your website. For example, you want people to know where you are located, how to contact you, and what types of clothing you are selling.

② Draw a picture of what your website's home page would look like.

③ Draw lines underneath it to the other pages on the website: for example, About Me, Clothing for Sale, Location, and Contact. You might have separate pages for different types of clothing: for example, Shirts, Pants, and Shoes.

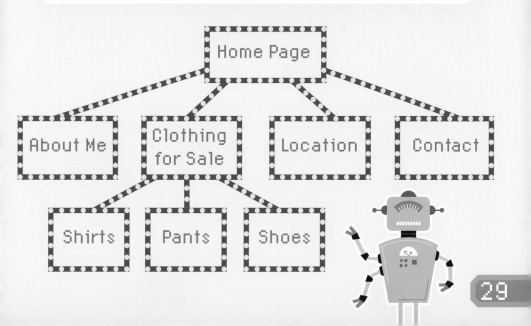

29

DEBUGGING CHALLENGE

Read the HTML code carefully. Can you match each line of code to the content in the box below?

CODE

```
<title>Miguel's Candy Shop</title>
<img src="swirlinglollipop.jpg">
<body>Come by Miguel's Tuesday Night
for New Flavor Night</body>
<b>Samples are free!</b>
```

MIGUEL'S CANDY SHOP
Come by Miguel's Tuesday
Night for New Flavor Night
Samples are free!

code (kode)
set of symbols that can be understood by a computer

fonts (fonts)
styles of type

logo (**loh**-goh)
a symbol that stands for a particular organization, company, group, or brand

navigate (**nav**-uh-gate)
move from one part of a website to another using links

programmers (**proh**-gram-urz)
people who write programs for computers

Bonus Question

What does <b> in the code do to the text?

Answer: It makes the text boldface, or heavy.

INDEX

FACTS FOR NOW

Visit this Scholastic website for more information on how to build a website:

www.factsfornow.scholastic.com

Enter the keywords **Build a Website**

ABOUT THE AUTHOR

Marcie Flinchum Atkins teaches kids how to use computers and find the best books in her job as an elementary librarian. She holds an M.A. and an M.F.A. in children's literature and lives with her family in Virginia. Read more about Marcie at www.marcieatkins.com.